MW00417191

Sarah Jefferis

WHAT ENTERS
THE MOUTH

Jessica —

So grateful for you.

Happy Holidays,

Sarah Jefferis

2020

Standing Stone Books
Fabius, New York

Standing Stone Books

What Enters the Mouth

First printing, 2017

Reproduction without express permission from the author or publisher is prohibited.

Standing Stone Books is a subsidiary of Standing Stone Studios, an organization dedicated to the promotion of the literary and visual arts.

Mailing address: 1897 State Route 91, Fabius, New York, 13063, USA
Email: standingstonebooks@gmail.com
web: www.standingstonebooks.net

This book is printed by Bookmobile, Minneapolis, Minnesota, and distributed by Small Press Distribution, Berkeley, California.

ISBN: 978-1-4951-9958-5

Library of Congress Control Number: 2016960070

Book Design: Adam Rozum

Standing Stone Books is a member of the Community of Literary Magazines and Presses.

For Ilah and Frida

*It is a joy to be hidden and
a disaster not to be found.*
–D.W. Winnicott

*The art of losing isn't hard to master;
so many things seem filled with the intent
to be lost that their loss is no disaster.*
–Elizabeth Bishop

Table of Contents

Dentist

What is it about the needle, the padding in the mouth,
the wild untamed tongue,

the metallic smell of cement
and tar, the drill, the masked woman

demanding breath, the chills,
the vacuum sucker,

the bite down here,
a little more, a little longer

that turns to a yellow sky afternoon
when my brothers bound

my pudgy arms to wooden posts,
cranked my mouth open,

and collected a dollar from every neighborhood boy
who would jam himself down

to my tonsils
how they begged me to swallow

how my brothers gave me
an Indian burn every time I bit.

How short the line from jaw to pelvis.
How even now I am in the chair

and on the ground watching.

I

The Buck

I slip in the poison ivy patch
same one I slept in

at seven when night walking
was easier than swallowing.

Fords rattle by, gun racks shine in sun.
Church bells ring. Noonday prayer.

Fife and Drum lines up,
turns, marches towards the Capital.

Trash bags squish with bug bombs
in overgrown grass.

Driveway: a sour tongue spitting
out a half-chewed Pinto on cinder blocks.

I think of sliding underneath,
calling for my brother to hide.

But he stares, spits Skoal
from behind the screen door

smiles while a buck charges
beneath the clothesline

stops short before my ribs are horn-split.
My mother's blouse caught in the buck's tail.

No, this is how it happens,
the buck lifts my little girl ribs,

splays me daily at my brother's feet.
Broken screen door smacks

with humid wind
the stench of us.

One Good Eye

After twelve hours on her feet at the gas station,
my mother, with one good eye, would pour
the water in, flick the iron on and wait.

She'd gather his blue or brown button-
downs, stiff polyester, and wrap them around the board.
This, the only time she unbuttoned his shirts.

The shirts he wore to make bombs at Lockheed
on the night shift. Roaches swung on the black iron cord,
leaping onto her King James or that book about Jefferson

and his mistress lying on a broken mattress. And how she
stared through the soiled window, the empty clothesline calling
her name. And why, why did I not offer to make the bed,

mend the clothes, silence the line with wet towels?

School Lunch

Before the Bible Verse of the day,
my name called on announcements,
Oh Sarah Beth, come down,
retrieve this, what I forgot on purpose,
what mama packed as duty.
I would have traded
my Slim Fast chalky chocolate shake,
my Wonder Woman thermos.
I would have sat closer to the spidery
lunch ladies with their missing teeth,
would have welcomed
the burnt turkey smell,
chewed old gum
married to blue cafeteria tables.
Just to see my monogram in lavender thread
like lace on Sharon's napkin –
hand stiched. Just to have
the crust of the cucumber
sandwich from her hand-made bread,
brown and seedy.

The Outward Visible Sign

The nits formed whole colonies,
planted flags in my head
as if the moon.

Mama used blue insecticide
shampoo day after day. Our ritual of TV
dinners, counting blessings, a hot metal comb.

Without a washer
she couldn't clean sheets daily
as the doctor recommended.

I slept sheet-less, on a plastic
mattress cover because I was
at 9 or 10 or 11 still wetting the bed.

My pee a lice pool.
A warning. An exit strategy.
A mark to keep them all away.

Infestations are trailings
of the gods, outward visible signs
of inward invisible truths.

Perhaps the pediatrician:
a man of bleached collar cloth
liked how I clutched

the paper or the feel of his finger
inside me. I never watched,
turned my head

to the wall and stared.
Could hear mama sigh
in the hall,

the lip of her
slip glistening against
the run in her stockings.

Play the Piano

Bootsie and I slept in a high bed,
my grandmother and I draped

in lace to match doilies on end
tables, lace over the Lord's book,

lace over my turkey legs.
She smelled of salty perfume.

Her husband slept in the other room
and she hired women

to turn and bathe him.
She never touched him.

His bed sores pink with puss.

I chopped pork fat for her collards,
and stole Little Debbie cakes

tucked behind Wonder Bread and Tab.
Her avocado kitchen sparkled.

No one was supposed to play
the upright piano in the corner,

for fear of cracking cherub statues.
Back in bed, her stepstool removed,

I counted beats between wall and mattress.
Every Sunday she would spank me

for leaving my prints on ivory.

How Grateful

I do not write about being the poor girl.
I do not write about sitting
in the back of the gas station laundry mat,
the heat of the dryer spinning
the yellow tables, the bent metal baskets,
counting change till
my mama gets off work.
I do not write about my mama
who postdates checks to cover
orange cream sickles, pigs feet,
Campbell's chunky beef noodle soup.

I vow to eat less.

I do not write about the flying roaches
or the constant unpacking and packing
of bug bombs. I do not write about
the flap of cotton sheets I hang
on the clothes line, how grateful I am
for the blood that finally came
at nine because it stopped my father's hand.

Moose Lodge

First time I caught my father crying–I was hunting
for my prayer-book and gloves in the room
divided in half by a shower curtain:

one half for big square computer screens
blinking. Floppy disks slipping off
a card table, behind the curtain sat plastic bins

of developer and the creaking black box with the giant eye.
I found my father in a closet pawing a photo of him and
his friend–or so he called him–in front of the Moose Lodge.

My father's snotty handkerchief balled up.
I should have turned away. Should have
called my mother. But I have never seen her touch him

on an ordinary day, much less a Holy one. I couldn't reach
him and couldn't step back. My crinoline stuck in white tights.
I pulled the Easter bonnet down over my eyes.

He made sounds I thought should not come from
a man. I don't know how I knew this. I wanted him to be more
dignified. It was not a quiet cry. This was the day he told me

the stone moved. And in those days I believed. Anything was
possible. I remember it every April when the burnt ham glazed
in sugar and maraschinos sizzles through me here, porch swung

and alone, I hear him wail for his friend who chose a wife.

Fake Crystal

I'd like to tell you what the bride's lips felt like
The truth of how I kissed the bride
And I could because this was the house of invention

where minutes before she giggled as she opened
thongs and hand mixers.
I giggled at the big banged bride to be.

Oh Aqua Net. O curling irons.
I'd like to tell you I was surprised by edges softened.
I'd like to tell you this was my first drink.

Mama fanned out carrots, Ritz, a cheese ball.
Poured more Kohl's into green sherbet.
An upside down volcano in fake crystal.

At thirteen, the punch bowl was my best friend.

Kissing Under the Loch Ness

Chalky slim fast slept in my Wonder Woman thermos
inside the blue locker with Ricky Schroder pinups
from *Teen Beat*. My first concert was Rick Astley:

a man with a mullet and white button down
who played synthesizer love songs.
First concert at Busch Gardens with my first boyfriend, also Ricky.

He drove a blue ford with a gun rack. Chewed Skoal.
A denim jacket, black jeans and cowboy boots.
My Ricky taught me to kiss while the other Ricky belted out flat.

My Ricky's hand on my throat;
he cut off my air. I still taste his tobacco
in the back of his truck in the parking lot of Busch Gardens,

the yellow Loch Ness Monster coaster twisting above.
Can still hear the wailing tourist's
right before they loop de-looped.

My Ricky spitting: *I can keep your breath, my Sarah Beth.*
He didn't have to be good. Neither did I.
I couldn't say it was Michelle I missed

in that moment, how her glossy lips in her hot tub
nights before and nights after invented me.

Beneath the Bleachers

At fourteen, it wasn't really about necks,
more like hands, six of them
fumbling all at once over buttons
and zippers and letter jackets.
I have never lettered in anything.

Never been to a game. Never been on the bleachers.
Only below. Daisies sprouting
in the uncut grass.
Never saw David Whitley tackle,
or kick. Robbie Deeds never touched David,

only watched how he held my wrists
above my head.
I would have done anything to get Robbie to watch,
my leg shaved mechanical pencil of a boy,
the shiny swim captain.

They were practicing for girls
they would take to prom.
The kinds whose mothers schooled them
in cotillion, who wrote thank-you letters,
who set the table each night,

lining the knives away from forks,
girls who still blush. Such good Boy Scouts.
I was the rope to practice knots.
I was the Sunday practice in the rain.
David kissed hard and sour,

left trophies on my neck. But Robbie,
a red head, the one I had played spin the bottle with,
the one who couldn't be in the closet was getting schooled.
I was his fish. I was the diving board,
the wall he flipped against, the water he breathed out.

Smile and Turn

Because you took black-and-whites
             in a field behind the drive in,
             demanding I smile and turn–

chin a bit to the left.
             My wings frozen with Aqua Net,
             My smile clamped beneath braces.

On daddy dates you took me
             to James Bond movies. Dropped your hand on my lap
             squeezed my knee when the girl
             in black velour mounted the spy.

I liked the Harleys and the long white cigarette holders.

You always asked me to scratch your back.
             Lifting your white T-shirt.
             Arm pits stained yellow.

You sat on my twin bed in boxer shorts–gap in fly.
             Yours not the first or last I saw.

I was an obedient child.
             Though molars and gums resist.
             My chin, wet with knowing.
Wet with knowing.

The Lesson

The chapel boy groaned
lust back in the bedroom

while my friend gave him head.
I was surfing cable channels:

watching *One Life to Live*.
Should have been excited,

she wanted to school me
and invited him next Friday, for my turn.

I should tell you I sipped
my first drink–a warm Watermelon

Bartles and James wine cooler. But I didn't.
My first dress rehearsal.

Learning to quiet my reflex.
I'd like to tell you I didn't go back

to her house. I'd like to tell you
I didn't enjoy it–

that I didn't buy new shoes
with the dollars he tipped me.

Under Fluorescents

I could have been my sister
tugging on my rhinestone stonewashed
tapered jeans. Not the skinny kind.

I could have been my cousin
whose husband came home from Iraq
and shoved his daughter's head

in the toilet every time
he thought she was someone else,
somewhere else.

I could have been my mother
scanning glue and plaster goblins
under fluorescents:

my nametag clipped to a red smock–
working eight-hour days to make
the lay-a-way payment.

But I stood in the long line
with my blue robe loosely tied in the back.
My panties and dress swinging in a plastic bag.

At fifteen I did what any man asked.
Signed my mother's name on the consent form,
I didn't tell her how her husband drove me here.

Three hours in stirrups.
The snap of the glove.
The sedative, dilation, aspiration and vacuum.

II

Not Sight

Who are we when a face opens to us?
A mirror, a compact funhouse.
A pond, algae green, or a reflection in drag.
A city to wear?
A map to fold in?
A well to fall down?
All of the women I have been are drowning.
Not a rope I haven't yanked on.

Who are we when a face opens to us?
Is it the other we attach to, or is it ourselves we see?
I have no illusions about who you are.
Or how you feel when you come. Or if you do.
Or how close a woman can get to you.
It is not sight I have lost.
It is how your face only opens when I am not looking.
When another calls your name.
How I know you pull her hair.

If I asked you to open your face
to me you'd laugh. I am startled
in the having to ask.
The request for permission.

Fourth of July in Williamsburg

You can no longer be arrested. I am finally eighteen.
There is only the Bishop to face and your own figure
in a gas station mirror. Key on a block of wood.

I am waiting for a postcard, a singing telegram,
a sign, waiting for frogs even to wallop the red dirt.
Waiting for you to swing on the tire.

Waiting for you to take Matthew Whaley's hand
and hopscotch on over. The dead boy chalking
maps of colonies on asphalt.

Virginia is always half of Carolina.
You are lighting up bottle rockets and cherry bombs
with your toddler in the suburbs, your lavender-shirted wife

swirling mint juleps on the deck.
No one can see the red light I am ringing
on your pager–it's next to sugar and ice cubes

shaped like American flags.
Somewhere another boy I am supposed to adore
is chewing Skoal and spiting in a tin before

he lights the grand finale for visitors
to witness masters and slaves,
oxen and sheep, *Fife and Drum*,

the basket maker, the apothecary,
all of America's crib burning.

The Modern Incubus

Like a night thief, you crowd
in my bed, already filled with Japanese
whining Sarah, *lay your sleeping*

head my love, human on my faithless arm,
and I have long since given up your skin,
your heavy wings.

In my arms, till break of day,
let the living creature lie, mortal, guilty.
On the line you demand

to know why I run over Jesus,
why I cannot let you be
you who will turn to river

dolphin during the day to bless and curse
those who ask for bread and wine,
you who framed my child self from bed to altar.

You, Beto, half siren cannot basket me
down the River James. Not back to the Parkway:
the road marked with Indians.

Nothing is ever entirely beautiful.
Maybe *a pot, a rare bit of trees,*
a tall treasure, a told tray sure, a nail, a nail is unison.

I did not call you here Father,
across the oceans,
I did not want the closed stale-

mate of a man promised to God,
a bird demon whose beak clips mine.

Tatami Mat

Woven straw to lay my futon on
Only to fold like a crepe
Offer up to the closet mouth

The sliding door
an accomplice
to all the understudies
substitutes
runner-ups
the Englishman who drinks gin with milk
the South African who calls me baby doll
the Japanese postman
all who rise and fall behind your handwritten letters
thumbtacked on the wall
blue envelopes, postmarks
not one asks
why I chose this high rise
this *fujiroukuchi*, this mountain mouth
far from the coast
Douzo yoroshiku–hajimemashite

I will say
I was keeping myself primed
rehearsing for the possibility of a box frame
a sleigh bed
a water bed
something off the floor
something that cannot be folded
a carpet
a two-car garage
a summer home on the Cape
another name
your name

each man after you
a familiar blade
a guillotine

Cycling

through the thousand-leaf city sleeping in cement
rebuilt after the war
one gray stone block
after another, the bastard
child called Chiba City

My *fujiroukuchi*, my mountain mouth
high-rise apartment walls thin
Senbei not even worth swallowing

English neighbors moan with sirens
speeding down the street too small to name
the sweet potato man
frying *imo* on the back of a bike

Train station street cleaner hunches over
his bamboo broom, brushes rocks
off dirt, clears a path for the cyclists
He is breast high
I'm the American he slows
down to examine:
Mite mite mite gaijin

He reaches to pet my hair
I want to bat his head with the broom
Onegashimasu, I say, meaning please
stop looking, please
let me pass through
to the temple   the bells ringing

obaasans hunch together
their wide straw hats brush–
these grandmothers tilt
wooden cups in the fountain
wash hands toss *yen* on the altar
clap three times to awaken Buddha

The Call

When I finally dialed, not drunk or high,
it was worth the way you said, *Ahh Sarah.*

As if you were still my Abraham.
I cannot imagine your new windowless office.

Nor see my sixteen-year old self climb in,
stilettos and Chinese take-out in hand.

Do you tell the groups you lead in basements
about me, do you confess my name

with instant coffee and donuts?
Your name a kind of salt water taffy rotting teeth,

your name a boomerang I have been casting
beneath every other skeleton who entered mine.

Surely all of them were not named Michael.

The heart you say *has its own algebra.*
And I did love you, though it was all shrouded in–

In lies I say. I must have sounded like a ghost.
What can T.S. Eliot offer you now,

and after all those years of my lessons,
you still can't explain the resurrection.

There is no evening spread against the sky.
And my spine has risen off the table.

And the women, the beautiful women, my dear
Father lover, how I make them come and go.

Maybe

For Heather

My stomach is five seconds behind
my mouth. My stomach tells me not to
but my mouth says sure, yes, absolutely.
But not with you. This is how I know
you are more than friend, how I want to take you
upstairs without the men watching,
and make you moan, want even to let you hurt me,
and then not run in the night. I say I might be
dating someone but he doesn't have me.
I don't have him. You tell me he does
have me and you wish he didn't.

Late Night at Denny's

Because we know a poor girl's dream
is the iPad Pro and a ticket to Tokyo,
is an ocean's hand of glass or a mussel
in a shell not yet open,
we sit late and into morning eating
seasoned fries and nachos
while Belgium explodes
on the screen above

or was it Paris, Egyptian air,
body parts floating in blue
above Airports agape.
We pretend we are girls, not yet mamas,

though we use words like *recapitulation* and *discourse*.
Call each other doctor
critique Chinese commercials
with dolphin soap.

You will return to your husband.
I have your shoe. I have lost
the godmother. Mice scare me more
each night. I will unlock a lost boy's house,

another who will never be just mine.
I want to make peace with this. He knows
no ticket can reach me the way you do
with your piano games,

your dtf blogs, the way you say,
dominoes and drinks on Tuesday,
the way you say
everyone wants to fuck you Sarah.

Ex-Pat News

When I heard across the wire,
dear Anne, that it was your brother
who stabbed you at the foot of the stairs

of your home,
poured gasoline around,
and lit up all the walls,

only to run down the cul-de-sac
and beg a neighbor to get the firemen,
I got out my own grill,

counted how many of your invitations
I declined to dinner. I couldn't be a triangle.
Couldn't compete with him for your affection.

I undressed poem after poem
about you and what had been,
could be, could have been

between us. The whole book.
Got a match, watched years of letters turn
black: float and fall.

Can't get those words to return
home no matter how many times
I light up my mouth with matches.

Answer

I.
Why the knife, dear brother, why the kiss in the kitchen
when she comes at night to your death row cell

did you want bricks or light
when you set her ashes on my palm,

did you wade in, forget the match, the gas
when the childhood house flamed behind you

did you beg all of her to sink,
when you tossed her shoes in the creek —

will you break off like a branch,
when you answer for this?

II.
I have shouldered her to every city
for the past twenty years

from Virginia to Japan and back.
Even my birthday belongs to her.

I have changed her sheets
made her bed. Have I not slept with her

more since she was dead? Alive
I could not bear her kiss.

August

For Andreas

In the spring you told me
all homes, all honeycombs have
an expiration date.
   The ending is
present from the start.
Waiting.

June lies
between us
lingers longer than three days
shoes on in bed
scarf around his head.

I knew. And still
July lies between us
an unexpected pig
burning in embers
roasting on a spit.
July wakes in a sweat
halves us, has us lie down across
the North Sea and Atlantic
too far from Heidelberg
too close to New York.

In the end your English lacks
all heart and all scales.
August renders more German
which is all feathered after all—

I could have carried what would have come
had you not walked in with vodka
and a morning pill
had you not left your centrifuge
flown back to Heidelberg
had you not chosen Katia
the skinny ugly one.

Quick Freeze Chihuahua Pop

You yanked your Chihuahua out of the freezer past
the Stouffer's Lasagna and Breyer's.

Rizzo you called her, had fainted, seized
in this Joshua Tree desert.
And we thought a quick freeze

would revive her, reincarnate her
Inner Great Dane. But she was in a sweat,
counting her inhales, not talking or blinking or barking

her musical numbers.
No more *Beauty School Drop Out*.
You thought CPR, and there's nothing like breathing

in a near dead dog to bring back two
lovers, but I was still hemmed in by the Chef.
I would be a liar if I said I didn't have mornings

when I would give up the chef to be on the back
of your Harley, from East L.A. to Santa Monica,
cradling *Rizzo*, on our way to the photo shoot:

all before you told me you didn't care for children
before you told me *don't swim one ocean for another.*

III

Reincarnation at the Kmart Intersection

I'm late to meet the doctor
and in the other lane
someone's grandpa tries to catch the light
and flips off his motorcycle,

rolls like a deer in the road.
I swerve around his red helmet,
think of another old man,
five years before at the same intersection,

how that bus driver stepped on the light,
and gave it all up
on the steering wheel of his number 30.
Witnesses hard as ticks. No one

willing to find a pulse.
Think of the driver not hunched over,
but waltzing on dotted lines with a partner.
He's trying to find someone

to share the salt with.
But I am on my way to make you, little risotto,
and I am late, and my eggs are only good
for a few more hours.

In my rearview, two green Ford trucks,
old ones, almost hit this grandpa,
and I think,
stop your car, you know how to find

the pulse, count the tango beats,
you know the breaths one needs
to keep the glaciers from melting,
the bees from dying, the levees

from dropping their lace like the slip
of the first woman you loved. That woman
who always said *I didn't mean to*
the morning after she had.

How she said this every Sunday before church.
Stop the car,
that's the priest you loved as a child,
still a fox. Be the Samaritan

your mother rehearsed in you.
Surely others will stop, others who fuck
on kitchen tables without once thinking.

Stop the car,
that was your specter of a father on the cycle,
the one who could become a grandfather,
the one who rides Harleys

through Florida everglades.
I swear I saw you,
my little risotto, standing
between bus driver

and motorcycle man, a hand in each,
them swinging you high.
I knew then how one cannot make one
if you pass by another.

The Pediatric Floor

I.
My first, three days old and yellow
as squash

left on the neighbor's doorstep.
I cannot leave her outside,

for lack of February light at her birth.
Inside, needles and IVs and little felt sunglasses

to protect the bulb above from burning her.
The incubator box she lay in, thick plastic

with a thermometer. Two tunnels for my hands.
Like lost rabbits.

She beats the plastic walls with her fists.
Wails, yanks the sunglasses off,

stares as if I have betrayed her.

II.
The second time, second child, same floor,
here after three days of groaning and Pitocin.

This is not her fire, merely my own
post-partum stomach beating the walls.

My pancreas dried and squished,
pleated. No stones.

Labor the reason.
Same nurses who replaced

those felt glasses years ago on her sister,
slip oxygen in my nose,

and dilaudid in me every three hours.
Engorged, I pour milk, thick

with fear down the drain.
My poisoned body drips.

Motherhood

I am holding the sun up
supporting a gas without a solid surface

while wearing leather gloves
with fox fur. Or mittens or rubber mitts.

My daughter interplanet Janet, a galaxy girl
travels like a rocket to her brother Pluto

and there has never been a planet she hasn't seen.
She sings lullabies to Mercury, pop rocks to Uranus,

ballads to Venus. But Pluto is my black sheep
prodigal, my god of the underworld

who won't answer calls, no matter how many hogs I roast,
how many sheep I sear, how many Technicolor

dreamcoats I stitch, how many miles I crawl
on my knees begging, my shins red, my knees starred

in a daily gravitational collapse: blue-black holes.
Still I hold up the sun. My hydrogen star.

My ring of fire. My near-perfect sphere.

Pink

Why is the elephant's vulva pink and swinging
my daughter asks, not loud enough for the zookeeper
to hear, or hundreds of faces pressed against

the wooden fence to feel wrinkly flesh.
As if the grassy hill behind laid its hands on us.
As if we were not all strangers, but family,

as if she was the hem of that famous garment.
We could be on our knees we want her to touch us so,
to touch her so–she could even heal us.

Ask, mama, ask, she eggs me on when zookeeper
chants about this grandmamma of a beast
and her many little elephants.

Babies are three feet tall and three hundred pounds.
This dry-skinned elephant with pink ears
picks up carrot, apple, candy even

with her prehensile nose-lip: her trunk,
the base, pink, grows hundreds of sensory cells,
perhaps more of a clitoris, pink too.

Last year, the one called Preya, drowned–
All other elephants tried to save her, in the end
they lay down in a circle wailing for days.

The Chilean flamingos, crimson and vermillion
alike, unlatched their beaks from bellies
and stared in disbelief.

They refused to eat.
They stopped switching legs.
Even the monkeys ceased to swing.

Learning to Spell

I.

When my daughter writes her name for the first time
gripping the blue pencil in her left hand,
saying across then down then across to make an I:
I see my mother's left hand and the nuns
who claimed the devil hemmed her in,
that she would have to use her right hand.
The left always a Judas.

II.

The police in Afghanistan
comb the streets looking
for women who have not covered their faces,
for women who meet with men
who are not their brothers or uncles or fathers.
They demand to know why one
had a coffee date, and surely she let
this other young doctor see her breast.
We were in public.
They want to prove she is a virgin.

III.

My daughter says you go down to make an L, and A and
an H. How an H is only an I in disguise on its head.
She is spelling Ilah, which means to bring calm in a storm,
calm out of chaos. Ilah, the cousin of Allah.
My little God watches me cry as she prints her name
again and again. Soon she will write letters from
the countries she can find on the map.

IV.

Some Haitian mothers jam
their own fingers into their daughters
to check their hymens.

My mother was a professional
patient who spent all day
with her size-six feet in stirrups,
teaching new interns to move in alphabetical order:
breast, cervix, uterus. She got paid
to let others practice.
Her flesh better than a plastic cast.

I can't tell you how I lost my virginity.
It wasn't my mother's hands
or the police or a doctor.
But I was at home, learning to spell.

Learning to Bleed

I know how to bleed.

I have practiced it for thirty years.
But in the pool of clotted blood in the shower
I wept for the ten year old in me who first saw

her own stain in shock and sorrow
and for the ten year old behind the door
calling out: *Mama are you all right?*

I am superstitious. I won't name a child
for someone who is still alive. I kiss
the top of a car when going over a drawbridge.

But last night when fistfuls of blood
came streaming out of me
I searched for your seahorse spine in them.

Held fistfulls up to the light, looking.
Though in the basement flood
years ago I lost you.

The First Sign

I sing to her of the red crane,

red only in face, but white in wing,
I sing, of how they are too light

to detonate land mines in South Korea. How a stream
of red and white glides like a kite in a rice paddy.

Even the soldiers hold their breaths.
This is the hour of the world without us.

My mouth is full of ashes, so are theirs, and yours,
and so too my daughter's when I tell her

the bees are dying. *This is the first sign*, I say.
The hives are collapsing, the art of simultaneity,

three, four hundred a month,
one after the other.

Hive Collapsing Disorder.
H as in home, my daughter says in the same voice

I have when I haven't slept for days.
I did not want to share my voice with her.

But she weeps as she hears of worker bees fleeing
the lonely queen, of farmers who claim

factory work when farms collapse.
Simply this, I must tomorrow sing

something lighter, a gliding lullaby,
a red river of sound,

something without these bones
I click under my teeth.

Hold Watch

I.
Hold watch child
for your one-eyed grandma

with rheumatoid, who demands pierced ears
and morning baptism.

She wants you to know
who you belong to.

Hold watch child, for she mails Jesus
with a crisp five dollar bill once a week.

II.
Hold watch child–
I cannot figure how to live with my face,

the wide cheeks, arched chin, German nose.
Remnant of those shaved and showered.

Even on you, I am drawing and drawn
and repelled. My little magnet,

my ghostly pane of prophesy
you teach me to see, and still

you must hold watch for her
in me, or for me in her, in you.

Moonwalk

My daughter eats English.
Chewing commas,
semi-colons, hyphens,

huhs, oh yeahs
the wheeeeees, the dammit
shit fuck honks–

with every pear dipped in balsamic.
More vinegar the better.
Honey too. She will catch all kinds of flies.

She will wear big hats so she is closer to Jesus.
She will food color the snow green
and plant silk birds of paradise.

She will ask who meant us to be.
She will count past three.
My running girl who does

the Michael Jackson moonwalk with one glove.
My girl who raises from the dead his ABC's,
singing on Free to Be You and Me

a duet with Roberta Flack: *I might be pretty;*
you might be tall; I like what I look like;
we don't have to change at all.

After Meatloaf

the dollhouse was the first thing the girls broke.
I wanted to hand them matches.
But what mother says *Yep:*
Go ahead, light the whole motherfucker up.

It will go soon enough. Wooden doors crinkle.
My oldest hammers each laminate floor.
Each wooden straw doll becomes kindling.
No use in making them think home was real.

Home is a kindling cage.
In the morning the mama
doll peeks out: a cyclops
with golden crispy hair.

What is not upside-down to two girls when
one mama says after meatloaf *I have had enough.*
I am done with you.
Backpack in hand.

I raise up our new house
one brick letter at a time
out of my spine and spit and blood.
I carry only the ones I birthed.

What I Cannot Face

For Frida

There are days when a woman I have never met bathes you, puts you to sleep. Braids your hair. Hair I made. Hair I grew. I am supposed to believe that anyone who adores you is good. That one can never have too many mamas.

But I don't.

I never wanted to share you, but to keep you from her who grills and sews and bathes you, would be cruel. And I know you are mine when you are six and tell me you want to skinny dip, when you refuse clothes, when I must tell you Barbie does not go in your vulva, when you say *bullshit*.

Forgive Me

Two years post-divorce and my daughter hands me her first poems. My hands shake. *Please,* she whispers, *for fuck sake don't cry.* As if my palms were signs, *my friends will see you.* She spits. *I am not crying.* I don't want her to write and I want only for her to write. I want another story for her, any other story.

I want her to be an architect, be the internal designer in her blood, the musician like her grandfather. I stumble on the rocking chair in the elementary school library. Stare at the rug with silver owls. Her poems want to untie ropes her mamas are knotted in, ropes that have knotted us. How can I tell her I was knotted before her breath.

Forgive me dear Ilah for calling you down from the stars ten years ago, for begging the dark to give you up. I have never wanted to share you to begin with. You were always and always not mine. Forgive me for breathing you in blood, for squatting you out, for giving you the flesh of a girl. Forgive me for teaching you the altar of verbs and how the only way out is to poem.

Night Walkers

For Ilah on her 11th birthday

What I want to tell you is to keep growing
despite the aching of I don't know,

I don't know how to build a home for you
but your other mother has a chocolate farmhouse.

I can house fourteen lines asleep
but can't shelter out rain and wolves.

I want you to be a nomad. A wanderer
who turns her nose up at owning land.

I want you to care more about who
rather than where. Where is always inconsequential.

The other night I found you sleep walking
folding three flights down in the laundry.

You and I are night walkers
and at two am you call out my name first

before you crawl in my bed.
It is not for me to save you.

Your body is yours.
I want to tell you to hold on for as long as you can

because everyone will want to purchase it, to own it.
Resistance, the only tale I can offer.

A Bee Flat Sonnet

I ate a honeycomb nest of girls inside a watermelon
left under an oak tree log. Couldn't swallow the queen.
All those who can sting will. All those who cannot, sing.
I grew antenna tongue and winged teeth.

Honeycombs still make me gag.
But hives inhabit every car I buy,
the latest: a yellow Toyota for three-hundred dollars
and thousands of miles with double-breasted

tuxedo nests in hood, in wheel, in pedals.
Been yanking stingers out of my heels for days now.
All those who can sting will,
all those who cannot: sing.

Sour

I cannot stand the smell of Sundays–
hot compost of them. Sundays sour

canker sore I run my tongue
over but can't quite see no matter

how many ways I open my mouth.
Sundays a fishbone trapped in throat

where even needle-nose pliers cannot reach.
Sundays a blue vase I shatter every seven days.

Sundays are Mary Queen of Scots who stepped up to the galleys,
stripped down to her bodice and gloves and smiled

at her executioners. Took fifteen attempts
to chop her head off.

Sundays a head that won't split from a spine.
Sundays the day I let my girls:

my blood mirrors-my ancestral ghosts
walk back to my ex.

Sundays the day of transition:
is like chewing roaches with wings and smiling.

Thank you Florence

You don't wear separation well. You want to fight over whose loss it is. You want to fight over the loss. You want the loss. You want loss to add to your collection. You want to wash it weekly. You want to pull it out, dress it up as a lawn ornament. You want to glitter it for your tree every December. Your hair has turned gray. The bags beneath your eyes thick like cement. You have hay fever. You were never one to cover up. The extra weight gathers your waist. Pounds have aged you. You and Florence are dragging the horse around. You can't bury it deep enough. The hooves keep kicking up daisies. And my neon name won't be written in stone.

What Divorce Taught me

People will not behave the way you want them to.
Including my children. Especially them.

Invisibility is the gateway to purgatory.
Sorrow is a choice.

Thoughts are fun house mirrors.
Invent and destroy illusions.

Not everyone loves to see what words can do and what they have to do.
Some people don't see words.

Bees singing in your brain will turn to ash.
Light the match every day.

Be both open and closed at the same time.
Don't choose.

Look stupid when you act
out of vulnerability.

Forget how to court ugly.
Beauty is a weapon you can now sharpen.

Be the granddaughter of the witches
who couldn't be burned.

Wanderlust courses through your veins.
Do not settle down.

Gather up the selves you left behind.
Each and every one laughs.

What Escapes Me

How the woodpecker recognizes
                    the tree to knock on.
How memory cells recognize
                    disease in blood and bone.
How they know the difference between
                    branches of adoration
And branches of disarmament.
                        How memory cells forget.
How cells scratched from the roof
                    of my mouth will panic
the way my own spine does when startled.

How the South clamps my throat
                    leaving her fingerprints.
How a whistling woman and a crowing hen
                    are an abomination to the Lord.
How after everyone
                    I have not filled
my pockets with fossils and crawled
                     into Cayuga Lake
calling out Virginia.
                    How the desire to flee burns.
How I kept a suitcase filled
                    with notebook and kettle and cash for fourteen years
but you're the one who left.
                    How after seeing your hand underneath
another woman's skirt
                    I still slept in your bed.
How each kiss begets another.

The Knock on the Door

I crave the hours that are unreasonable.
I'm building my new home with them
though I can't stop hammering my thumb.

Unreasonable hours stronger than the foul breath
of a wolf woman in a chef's coat.
Hours stronger than the colonial bricks made from oyster shell.

Only these hours will guard my wild willing stupid heart,
the one always ready to show her spirit under the fans,
to show her knickers really.

I intend to trade in my heart for one more refined–
one with a better rhythm,
a new chamber cave that won't recognize your call

or every time you sing that song, our song–
and who will refuse the oven that called out Plath.
I am not Sylvia, not this year, but I know that

the faces of her children were not enough.
I intend to trade in my heart for one more discerning
who will know if the knock on the door belongs

to Judas or Elijah. Though they sound the same.

My Last House

I don't believe in the law of attraction.
I didn't attract poverty or the monster

who came three times to my house
leaving shit, whiskey and cirache in my kitchen.

He took the extra key,
two hundred dollars, and my daughter's computer.

Left a note on my bed about how I should bend
over and then swallow. I don't know his handwriting.

Even the police tell me I can't burn the note.
They sit outside my door and wait. Watching. Moving.

I want to believe I deserve
a job that pays the bills,

a lover who wants to hold only me,
a house, a night without waking.

Until Saltwater Fills Me

As a child, mama put me to bed with a fairy tale:

A girl in a stadium with lions behind her
and three doors. Behind one door is the man God

intended, behind another the ocean,
and the third will not open.

I could never choose the correct door.
Door handles make me nauseous.

I dreamed of crawling in the lion's mouth.
I will a cyclone of wind and an orange sky.

I will drive and drive until saltwater fills me.
My other body is the sea.

I will teach my girls how to be a housewife
is to tape one's mouth twice.

I will give them Kahlo so they know

leaving is not enough
they must stay gone

their hearts canvasses
they can paint

without lions or doors or any man
God intended. A lion's mouth is a cleaner savior.

I will have men and women who are contained in the hours
they appear. I will make them disappear.

I will have hours ahead and before.
I have given up on diamonds,

traded them for metaphor,
the only lover I will strip for.

Please Leave Immediately

Please leave immediately my dear I want to take you in the hallway.
Keep you where you belong. On your knees. On your knees I can keep
you. Everything you need is here. I am a bottom tweeter. Please leave
immediately. I have a crush on all of you. My long forgotten tribe. My
love poem requires a smoothie and Seymour Glass and a couch you don't
want to put your face on. The body is miraculous. The goal of this is not to
let the lack of success as a dater be too obvious on the page, so please for
God's sake leave immediately. The greatest poem is the human nervous
system. Please leave immediately or else I will harvest your tongue. Just
leave immediately. The intellectual anatomy of I am says I am not not yet
immediately. Leave. Please is a gossip column about my body and a plot
horror. Please leave immediately I am a master curator. No I did not say
the other. But that is also true. Come with me to the monster. Come to the
monster. Come my monster. Come monster. I know your name. Please
leave epistemology immediately. Please leave immediately. You are hereby
permitted to all men. All men are hereby permitted to you. Please leave
immediately I am trespassing gender on genre. Don't make me choose. I
go walking after midnight.The scar on my tongue has my father's name. I
have not spoken to him in twenty years. For this I will cut myself open. The
obvious considerations are touching so please leave immediately. Oh White
Whale. You can't libel the dead. When you find us all we will be gone.

Horoscope for the Sagittarius

You are walking through glue and tar. Your feet are stuck, your knees stuck. You would walk on your hands if you had the strength. But you are fresh out of it. You hate the women who pay for cross fit. It sounds like Jesus jumping with the cross on his back. You have been cross or fit but never both at the same time. Mercury is in retrograde. You will do whatever she wants. You will call for tea and be rejected. Don't call. You will call for someone to check the windows and have to leave a message. No one will come. Not even those in uniform. Not the nurse who claims he wants to protect you. He has made you more confused. He has taught you to love no one but yourself. Glue yourself up. Don't keep ironing his scrubs. Say no often. You will say the triple mantra every morning, noon and night, when you loose your keys, when you walk with them in your fingers, listening behind you, when you unlock the front door afraid again of whiskey, shit and cirache. *Aad Guray Nameh. Jugaed Guray Nameh. Sat Guray Nameh. You will bow to the truth that has existed throughout the ages even though you can't see it. Bow to the invisible.* Hoping even she won't abandon you. You try not to cross yourself. Your daughter will tell you she is having a breakdown. You will call it a spiritual awakening.

IV

On Your Island

Growing up on food stamps meant
I didn't know imitations were imitations.
The stamps slept in my mama's blue
plastic Penney's wallet right next to
real dollars from hours on her feet
at a gas station. Imitation potatoes
in a red box. I swallowed milk she added
water to and ranch dressing on iceberg.

Arugula with balsamic in brick houses I never knew
so all my loves have been chefs. You turn
avocado into guac and I'll be on my knees–
Roasted sweet potatoes will have me undoing
buttons before I am asked. I will blow a stranger
to keep my daughters fed.

In line at a food pantry, in the sea of abandoned wives
who believed in happy endings, I cannot tell
you where I stood before I met you and dates
that come with breakfast dumplings and ackee.
I want to not want to eat your
food. If I eat your island, put your country
in my mouth, I will change my passport. Escape
routes are bloodlines. Heart is tongue and my belly
the first to fall. Let us not eat together.
It's the only way.
I can stay.

This is Me Following, or Raisin Bran and Strawberry Lube

I.
You love pussy the way I love metaphor
and the cock will trot out without the heart
daily if it can, and now and now and now–

And now the floor drops when you lift
me on your kitchen table in full morning light,
the water from your fish tanks humming
and your mouth between before I can even breathe.
Coming is a place you keep me in,
contain me: to have and to hold.
I want to not want to be containable.

II.
And metaphor trumps the narrative of us,
"us" a word you uttered,
a word I stumbled against but this
is your love poem, your anti-love poem,
better than cupcakes or roses
or any other token
of affection from your waiting list.

This is about Raisin Bran and Wal-Mart kiwi
and strawberry lube and batteries
and bowties and curtains on sale
at Bed Bath and Beyond.
This is about touchdowns and stompers and lickers
and individual hair dryers, previous pussy erasers, and video games
with other ridiculous girls with larger than life tits.

III.
This is for the boy who was raised up
by a great-grandmother or taken out for talking back.
This is for your mama
who left the island for the States,
and how she longed for your face
each time she soothed another mama's child.

This is for the eight-year old boy
who stumbled off the plane at JFK.
You were a man in little bones not knowing
you were black till your feet hit American soil
the stench of the Bronx clogging your pores.

This is for the young adult who
studied up and down the spine of America
only to pass her test, to promise allegiance.

IV.
This is gratitude for the dumplings and cornmeal porridge.
This is for the ackee and catfish I have yet to devour.
This is for the moment when we were dancing
to Sarah Vaughn and you wanted me to follow.
This is me following.

This is for the afternoons when you surprise me at my house
and for the three and four times you call a day.
This is for when I know
you are conquering the body.
Someone else's Body.
And you have left for the City in search of
wealthier pussy to colonize.
You want me to be an island.

And my resistance bothers you.
I'm searching for a pedestal on which to stand
above your ridiculous chorus line.

This is how we bend
the possibilities of metaphor,
tie her down and spank her,
to make her behave.

And now I clutch the bed rail, the kitchen table, the park bench:
which is made of wood and so it gives,
which is large enough for all of us.
My legs wrapped around you. The geese cawing in the background.

V.
Simply this: I offer you the art of the open hand–

I want to stand in the bathroom and watch you shave.
I want to make you breakfast.
I want to not want to make you breakfast.
I want to not want you to say: "Honey, I'm home."

Needle Pulse

When you touch me do you replicate all the lions before you
or draw them out to behead them.

When you touch me do you feel the bowl
of fish and chocolate spinning my head.

When you touch me do you know I lived for years
without this because I had girls

that I gave up touch for family.

When you touch me do you hear all the football players
who took turns beneath the bleachers.

When you touch me do you see my brother's friends
who tied me down in the fort.

When you touch me I don't split in half
I don't witness the Sarah's before

or call out to the year I wanted to be Beth.
There is no one wrestling an angel. No one asking for a blessing.

When you touch me I am not transported back
or shoved forward when you touch me I am rooted.

Branches grow in places I didn't know possible.
In daylight I can bare almost anything.

Slippery

Killing every vagina in the neighborhood you oddly, as a I lay next to you, sweaty and swiveled and swooned, look at pictures of a blonde whom you swooned when her husband wasn't home, though you say that wasn't your preference, secrets not your game, and I want not to give a shit, or feel a little unhinged but I would be lying. And I am many things, but not a liar. I'm not the jealous type. You offer me a slice of cake from another woman. I refuse at first. You say you don't attach emotional significance to objects the way I do as you rehang your ex's shower curtain strewn with palm trees. Is it a grand invitation for her return? Let me stencil your bathroom to welcome her in. Of all those on your waiting list, maybe I would like her the most. Though her renewal would be my exodus. Things may just be things for you. Objects of affection. You claim to be romantic but you are slippery as an eel. I have not determined if you are good for me or trouble or maybe a little of both, I know I can be someone new and old with you, someone I haven't seen in years. You quipped while cleaning the bathroom on my birthday how I was one iota above casual and I wanted to walk or spit. Making me dumplings and jerk chicken, you offer a Frida Kahlo exhibit in the city in April, if you can imagine me in the Spring. The push pull. I know you are here for me not to hold my tongue. How I hate you under my skin. And I want you nowhere else.

Riddle Me Now

Tell me a storylie
and in Caribbean time I will learn
the lean boy from the man.

Give me the islands you have inhabited–
and the arrows you left there.
Give me narratives from your life before.

Riddle me now
in morning light
on the kitchen counter and in the shower.

Riddle me now and now
And don't assume I am without plans.
I have plenty.

I dream big and alone.
Riddle me now and now but believe
I am not your sweet spot.

You tell me the only thing better than one–
is more than one.
You think it's about happy moment making.

It's not that easy.
I can do that with batteries.

To get over you I ate straight from the fridge
for five days: curry chicken legs, rice and beans
and whiskey, neat. Only to banish bones.

Nothing has ever been licked clean.

13 Ways to Get Over Your Lover

Pitch the coffee mug
he bought from the island.

Give up coffee entirely.
Refuse ackee. Leave the plantains

at the market. Let the curry go.
Unleash the goat.

Put down the chicken.
Whistle and whistle the crowing hen

back to its own abomination.
Be the abomination.

Scald the pots he bought.
Let the knives go dull.

Give up riddles and rum.
Swallow the literal.

Let the dominoes grow dust.
Hurry the hour.

Let the orchid choke.
The mangos rot.

Call his other girlfriend,
the one you fucked for him

and sometimes for yourself
tell her it was all fun

till the floor dropped out
beneath you.

You have never longed
for a floor till now.

Even Hands

Sink holes open up between
what I said and what you heard.
I am on borrowed
time. I am not a great believer
in luck. You hear I have time
and are lucky to be
with you. We bring our own
interpreters to the conversation.
Even hands cannot spell.
Fingers overtime.
To love someone is to murder
interpretations, or perhaps to clean ears,
to listen as if our lives depended
on it, to stop hearing what we want
to hear, to stop, to pay attention.
To translate requires a kind
of ceasing and the canyon
in your bed where I risked enough
to say *I live in the land of not like*,
and how you replied you were always mine.

Riddle Me Again

I am not your burning house.
You can't rush back in and get what you forgot.
I am not the car wreck or the lost rear view mirror.

Not a horse to be tamed.
Not a crossword puzzle.
Not an alphabet for you to learn.

Not a mat for you to practice on.
Not a fence for you to sit on.
Not waiting for you to choose.

Not a chess piece for you to move.
Not your boy.
I am not invisible and not made visible by your stare.

I am   the other   in the room.
My alone feels so good.
And I will, as Shire said, *only have you*

if you are sweeter than my solitude.

When He Calls

Remember how he reminds you that he could have not come at all. That he said 3:30 and arrived at 6:00. Remember that he said if he could be late he would. Remember how you hold time as a sign of respect. Remember how he takes two steps forward just before he disappears. How disappearance unravels you.

Remember how in the kitchen he didn't move towards an apology. How he made food, packed boxes, and you saw his two step shuffle. How he said everything about you was out of balance. Remember how you wanted to kick him. How he thinks you were passive aggressive. How you didn't want to be his mirror.

Remember the moment in his car at the park, how he said, "I'm fucking you. Not making love." Remember how you asked him to kiss you because you wanted to fight close up. Remember his resistance to argue. His resistance to stand outside of language. When all you wanted was a sentence.

Remember he said you were the one he couldn't understand. Remember how he made you come and go. His four am fist on the kitchen table. Remember how he fucks you knowing you will write this.

As If

To acquire speech we have to exhume ourselves. Speech cannot arrive with breath. This blue in my exhale is not only my blue. All the world clatters and chimes and babbles. For many years I answered to a different name. What shall you call me? Even the poet said: *There are voices that wake us in the morning and voices that keep us up all night*. Which are you? I want you to touch me as if you want to know me as if you have always known me as if in the knowing I have become your the, and you are my I.

The Two Archers

I am the contradictory one
who turned around at six months and twelve.

I am not good at letting go.
I had to repeat the dress rehearsal, the opening act.

And you, my Vera, do a two step
forward and back shuffle

that would make Nabokov and Humphrey green.
I can't stand in constellations for long.

I preempt the ending.
Leaving always before the breakdown.

I could tattoo our constellation on my ass.
But I am not, will not be property.

The cue cards and the old Muppets in the black box
tell me the show is over. Or it shall go on.

Either way there is blood and orchids,
boxes packed, couches that don't fit through doors.

And kitchen counters and park benches and toy stores.
And your silver cardigan I can't get out of.

And lust enough that friendship is impossible.
That yacht sailed the first time you kissed me at the lake.

You can't unkiss someone.
You undress sentences in full adoration.

You have turned and turned me on a spit.

What I Have and Have Not Invented

My age, my weight, who I was with last night.
That I didn't like women. That I did.

That I can be kept. That I belong to someone.
That I want to belong to someone.

That I stopped believing in the fairy tale. That I still do.
That I want you for myself. That I don't care

about the chorus line of blonde women ringing you.
That I was the priest's secret.

That three times before the age of twenty, I took my own life
in my hands, knotted and wrung it by the throat

to choke it quiet, still. Lies behind, lies
within desire, wants forming like volcanoes,

if I say it, surely it will arise. I am a fabricator.
A narrative slut.

A perjurer with tongued artillery. One who polishes
sentences, spits and buffs them till they shine.

Notes

Page 35: The Modern Incubus

And lay your sleeping head my love,
human on my faithless arm
But in my arms, till break of day
Let the living creature lie
Mortal, guilty.
    – **W.H. Auden**, "Lullaby"

A pot, a rare bit of trees, a tall treasure, a told tray sure, a nail, a nail is unison.
    – **Gertrude Stein**, "Susie Asado"

Acknowledgments

I am thankful to the literary journals who have published these poems in earlier forms.

"Learning to Spell," *The Patterson Review* (2nd Prize, Allen Ginsberg Poetry Award)
"Reincarnation," *The Healing Muse*
"One-Eyed Ironing," "Molding My Father," and "Aural Lesson," "The Dentist,"
"School Lunch," and "At 14" "What I Wish to Take Back" and "Smile and Turn,"
Ithaca Lit.com
"Motherhood," *Stone Canoe* (Winner of the Bea Gonzalez Prize)
"Bee Flat Sonnet," *The Moth*
"Slippery," in *Boys and Girls (Anthology)*, Luna See Press
"This is Me Following," *Rhino*
"The Outward Visible Sign," *The Aperion Review*
"The Call," and "The Modern Incubus," *From the Fingerlakes (Anthology)*
Cayuga Lakes Press

I am grateful to the Saltonstall Foundation of the Arts, the Community of Writers at Squaw Valley, and the Colgate Writers Workshop for providing me with time and space to complete this manuscript.

I am grateful to my professors and mentors at Hollins University, Cornell University and SUNY Binghamton, particularly Maria Mazziotti Gillan for all of her encouragement and compassionate guidance.

I am indebted to all the actors and teachers in Actors Workshop Ithaca who kept offering me repetition and laughter, but especially for Marissa Biondolillo, who required me to own my own shit, and taught me how to live truthfully in imaginary circumstances.

I am grateful to Karyn Young, Katie Rice, Christa Nunez, Elizabeth Lawson, Chris Sgroi, Cathy and Frank Zimdahl, Jaya Lalita, and Mame Cudd, for their constant belief in my writing and for helping me find my calling.

I am grateful to Heather Dorn and Jose A. Rodriguez, fellow poets and SUNY graduates, who read countless versions of this book, who witnessed my process and didn't turn their heads to the wall, whose line edits and insights motivated me to keep writing.

I am thankful for Blayne Stone, and all the moments he told me not to sit on gold.

Praise for Sarah Jefferis' *Forgetting the Salt*

"*Forgetting the Salt* is an astonishing collection of poems, packed with love and fury, irony and humor. Tough, urgent, surprising, these poems are both necessary and comforting."

 – **Maria Mazziotti Gillan**, Director of Creative Writing at SUNY Binghamton

"In *Forgetting the Salt* origins meet with exhumations that wring from their vital truths. In these poems, to remember is to want to forget, and tensions between formal and free verse define a line the poet walks from bondage to escape and expansion. The nuclear family—severed—sets the stage for the human family's failings on a larger scale, yet there are redemptions of connection, of the telling itself. The last lines of these poems ring like clear bells."

 – **Cathryn Hankla**, Director of Creative Writing at Hollins University

"Sarah Jefferis's poems in *Forgetting the Salt* combine dazzling metaphor with an undiminishable lyricism; here is a twenty-first century Romantic worthy of the calling. In her poems, one encounters a mind that dallies with the surreal, and yet always returns to the terra firma. Like the poet Ai with whom she shares so much, Jefferis's poems sparkle with their old associations and radical suffusions—in one marvelous poem, a pyromaniac, "harvests the sweet flames" as all is engulfed. In another lyric, we contemplate the gestation period of an elephant, finding in its protracted struggle our own rude calculus. Jefferis, thank goodness, astonishes as she delights; and yet, and always, there is a wise woman-centered sassy spirit. If she has traveled far from the church, she is never far from revelation. This is a stunning collection of poems— smart, elegant and yes, fiery."

 – **Kenneth A. McClane**, W.E. B. DuBois Professor of Literature at Cornell University